CONSERVATION TALES

Bats

Stories of wildlife conservation for beginning readers

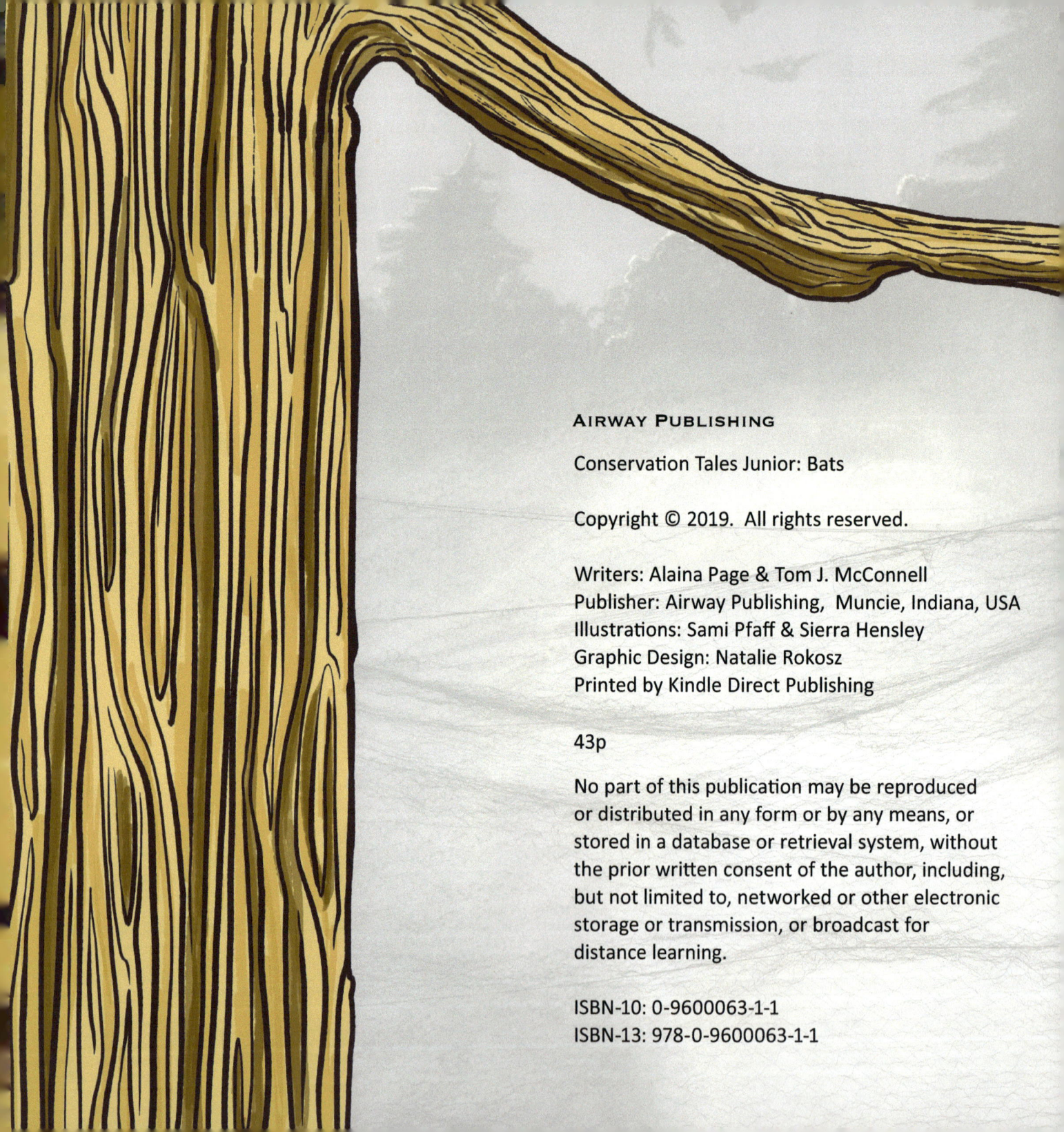

Airway Publishing

Conservation Tales Junior: Bats

Copyright © 2019. All rights reserved.

Writers: Alaina Page & Tom J. McConnell
Publisher: Airway Publishing, Muncie, Indiana, USA
Illustrations: Sami Pfaff & Sierra Hensley
Graphic Design: Natalie Rokosz
Printed by Kindle Direct Publishing

43p

ISBN-10: 0-9600063-1-1
ISBN-13: 978-0-9600063-1-1

For my mom, who has always been my biggest supporter and inspiration.

Alaina

To both of my sisters Sara and Megan. While you both drive me crazy sometimes, I am so blessed to have you both in my life.

Natalie

Diana sat by the evening campfire. In the faint light of the dusky sky she saw something little soaring in the air.

That is a bat! Bats come out to eat insects at night.

Camp counselor Jenna walked to the edge of the forest to get a better look.

Tajana was nervous. She thought bats were creepy and scary and maybe even dangerous!

My brother said bats are vampires!
Don't worry! They won't hurt us. We want bats in the forest. We try to make a good home for them here.

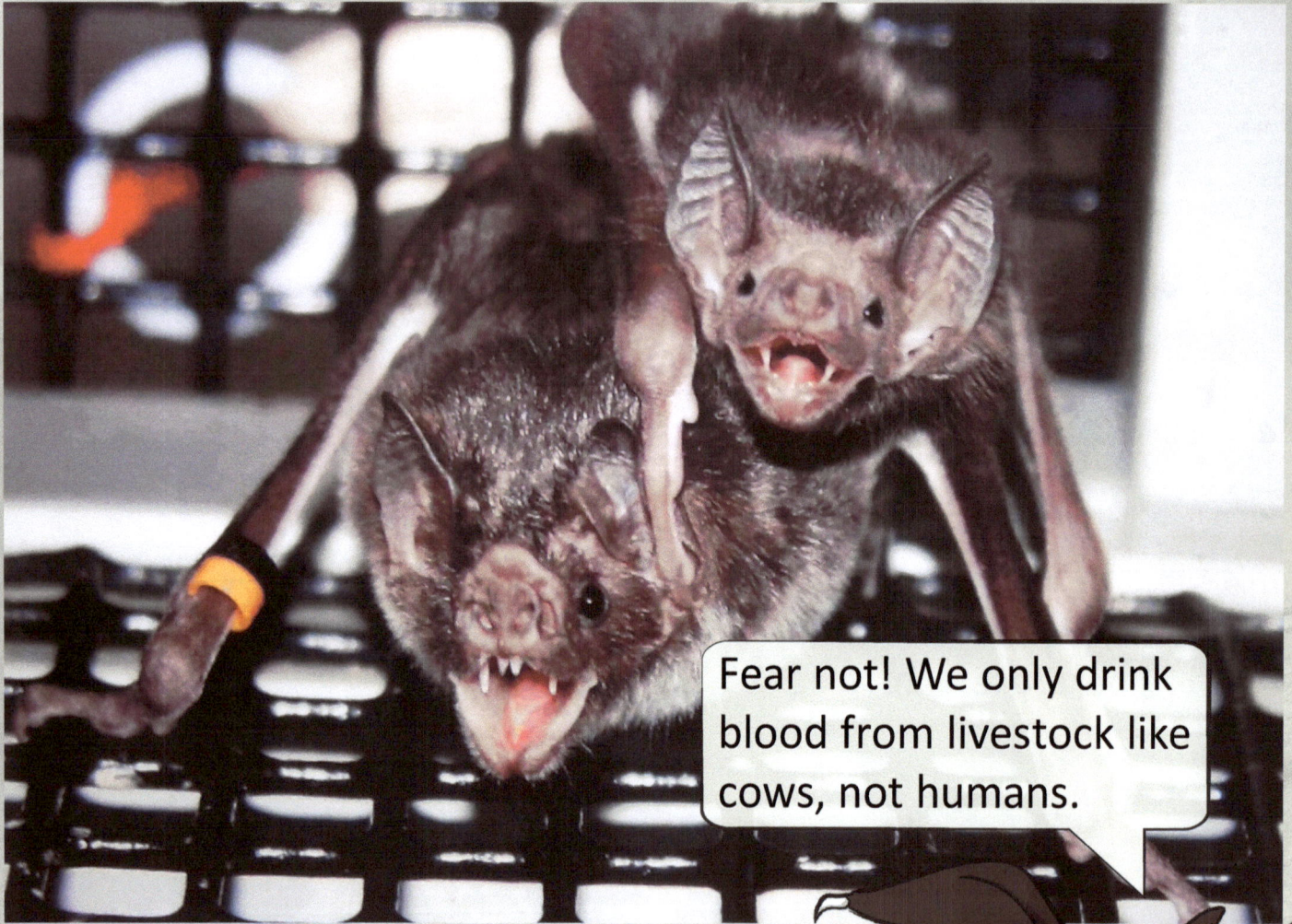

Speech bubble: Fear not! We only drink blood from livestock like cows, not humans.

Vampire Bat (OBC, 2016)

Vampires aren't real, but vampire bats are! And it's true: they drink blood! There are many different species of bats, too. Each species has its own unique characteristics.

Eastern Red Bat

Little Brown Bat

Northern Long-eared Bat

Some bats have ears twice the size of their heads. Others are about as little as a bumblebee. But bats are in danger of disappearing forever! Scientists help protect bats.

During the day most bats sleep upside down.

At night bats fly around eating pests, insects like beetles moths, and mosquitos. Mosquitos can spread diseases to humans. We need bats to help us keep the pests away.

The next day, the campers
went to the nature center to
learn about the research that
scientists do to make sure bats
can live in the park.

Diana had so many questions.
How do you study bats? What
were they trying to find out?
Did they do experiments
on bats?

The scientists had a lot of tools.

Thick Yellow Gloves

Rubber Gloves

Bat Detector

Ruler

Hanging Scale

Bat scientist Kristi smiled broadly. She was excited to share science with the children. "Would you like to help us catch some bats?"

Kristi led the campers on a short hike through the forest. They came upon a rippling creek where they joined two other bat scientists. Kristi immediately began helping set up a net.

We are going to catch bats, measure them, check them for disease, and tag them for our research.

The campers watched while the bat scientists put up nets made of soft threads.

Everyone put on headlamps as the sky darkened. Soon, the forest was lit only by moonlight.

Look! They're starting to come out! Now all we have to do is wait for one to fly into the net.

Big brown bat in net

Hours passed and the net remained empty. Diana thought she would burst if she had to wait any longer. Finally, Kristi called out, "We caught a bat!"

Kristi grabbed a pair of rubber gloves and carefully untangled the bat from the net.

Kristi explained, "First we find out what species the bat is. You can tell by looking at its face, ears, size, and fur color. This looks like a female big brown bat."

The scientists measured the bats wings and weighed it on a scale. They need to make sure bats are growing, just like your doctor does. Tim wrote down the measurements on a chart.

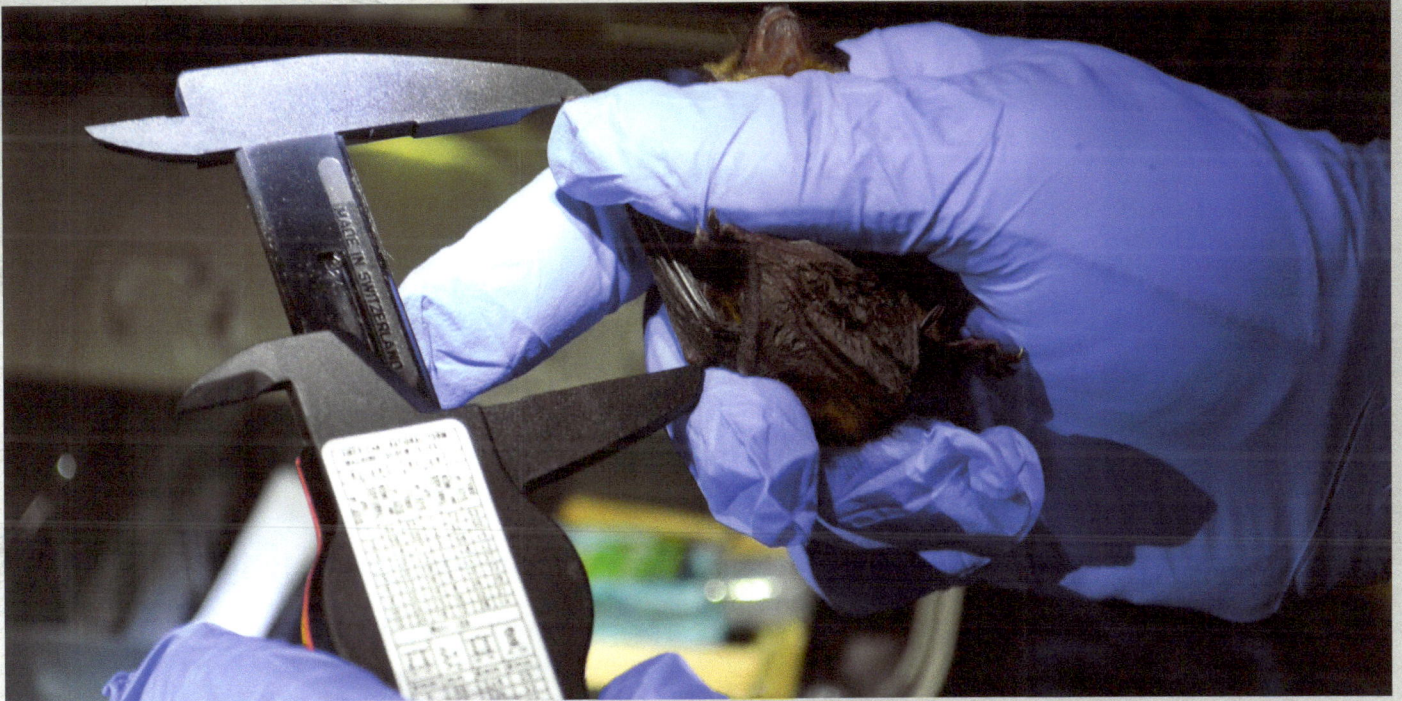

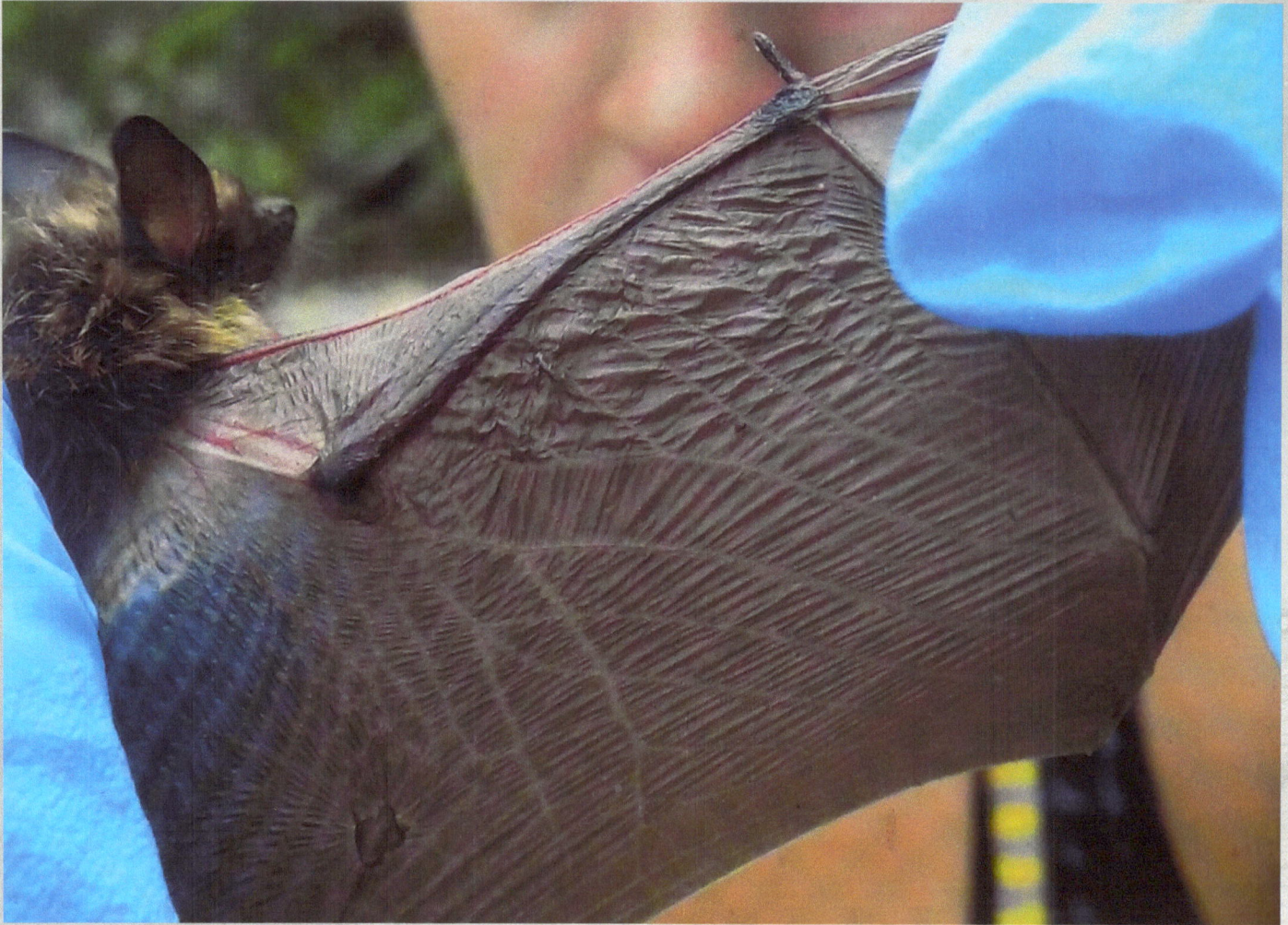

Kristi stretched open the bats wing and studied its skin. "Diana, write on this chart that she has a scar on her wing. It could be a sign of white nose."

White nose is a disease like the flu, but for bats. It is a fungus that infects bats and spreads very quickly.

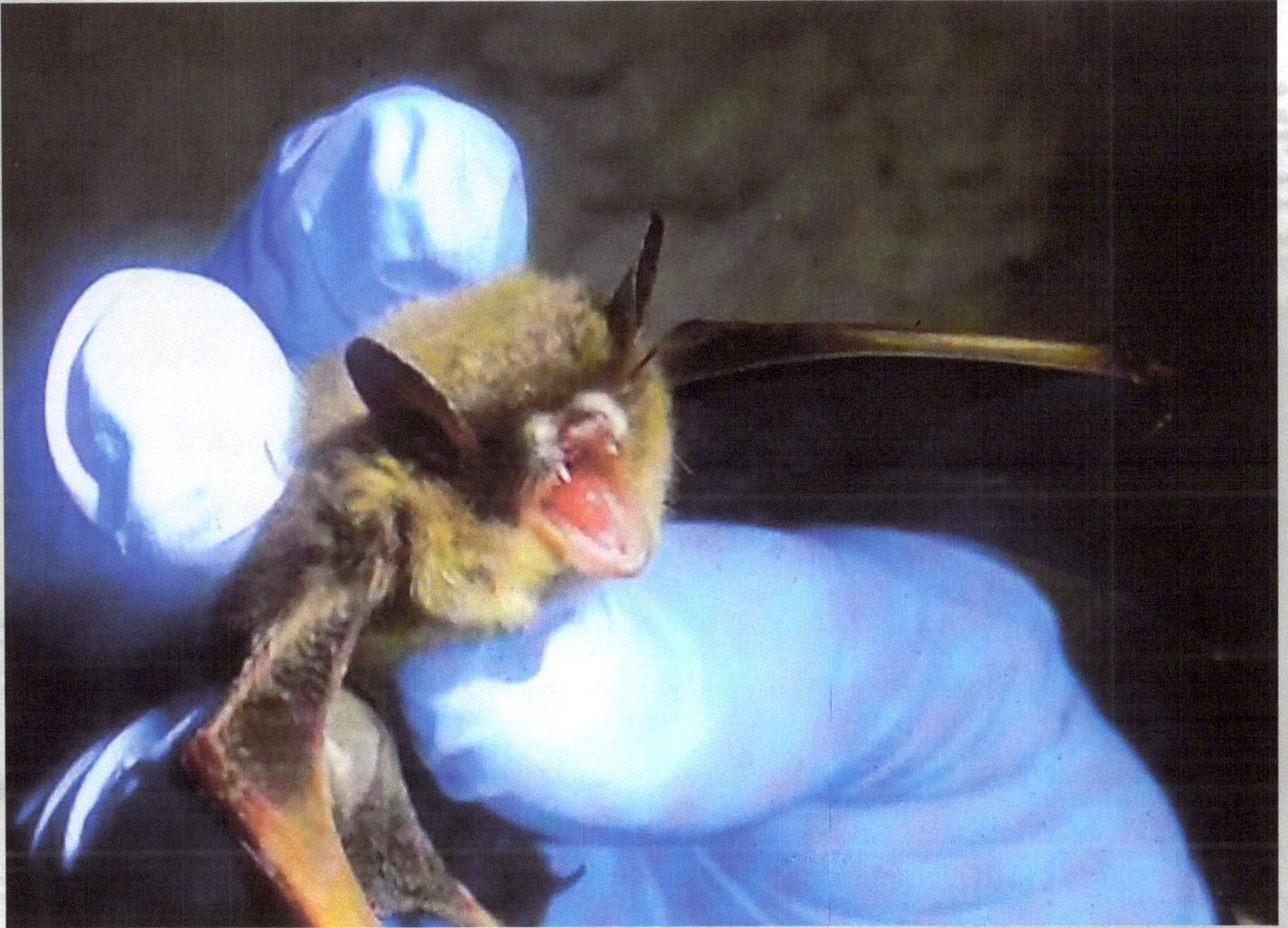

You can tell if a bat has white nose by looking for scars on its wings and white mold on their face. If one bat in a colony gets it, it can spread and kill most of the bats in the area. It's one of the main reasons why bats are endangered.

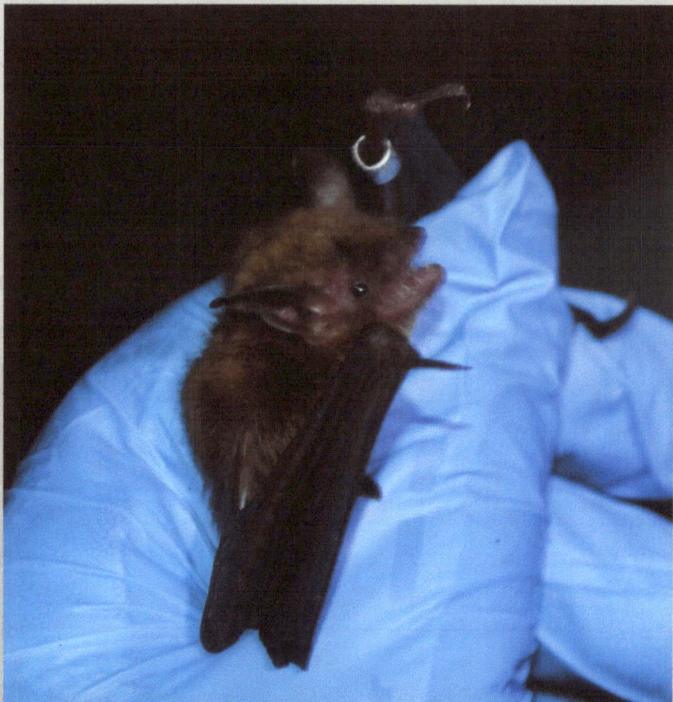

But scientists can help! Kristi explained that to help stop white nose, scientists tag bats and monitor their movements. Tags are metal bands with numbers that scientists attach to an animal, almost like a nametag. That way, if the animal gets caught again, scientists will know who it is.

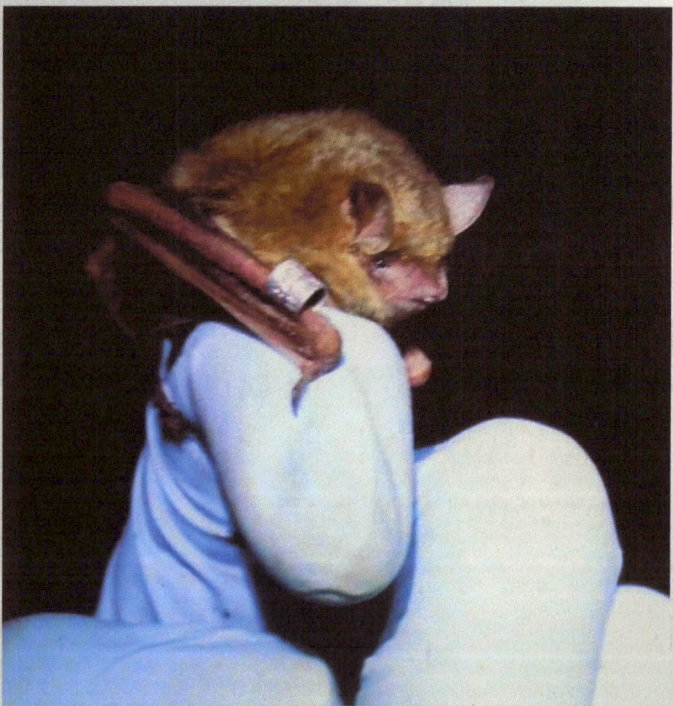

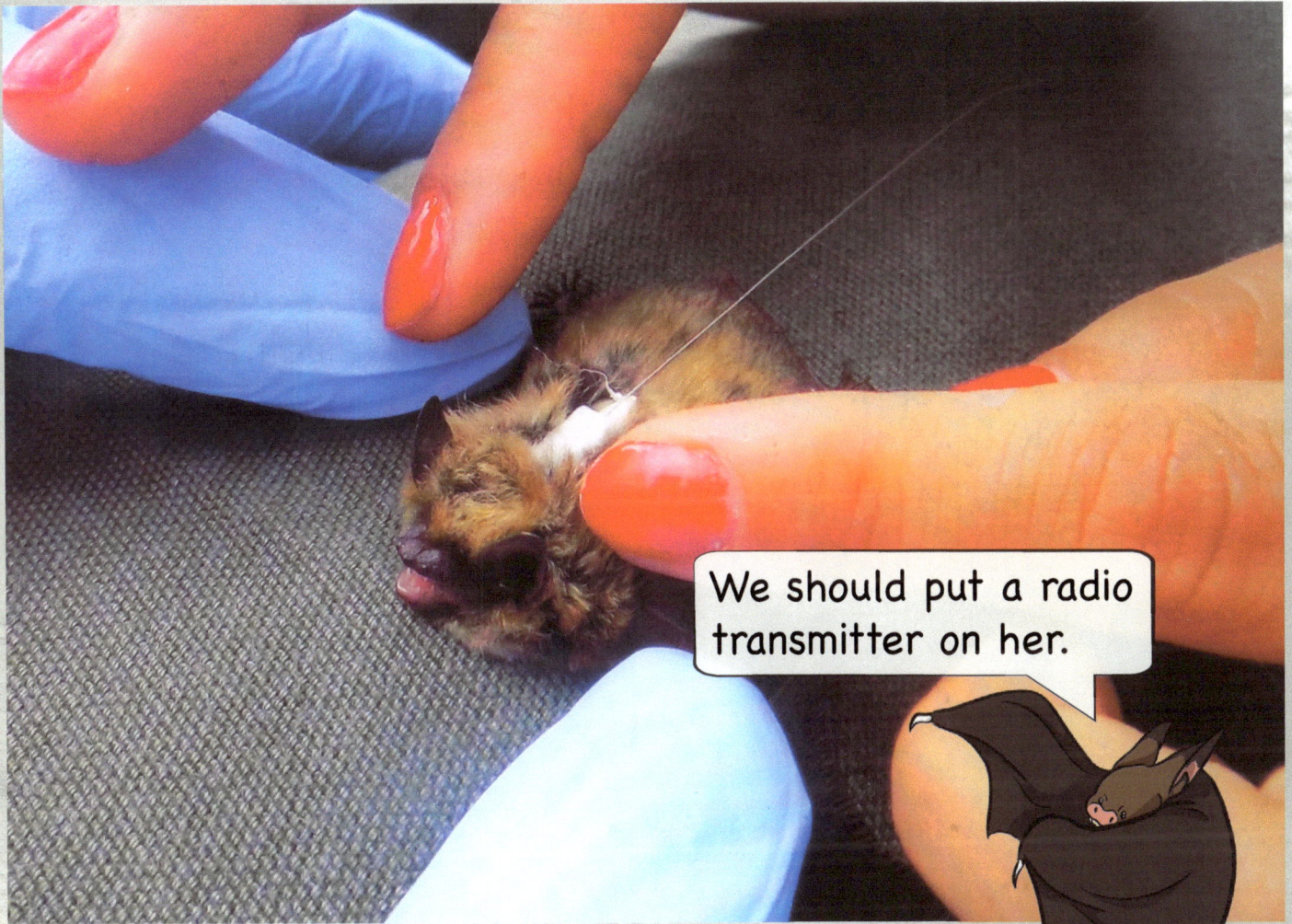

We should put a radio transmitter on her.

Mounting transmitters on bats

Kristi gingerly trimmed a patch of fur on the bat's back and glued a transmitter to its skin. With a radio transmitter, scientists can track where a bat is using a computer.

When Diana woke up the next morning, all she could think about was helping bats.

Jenna said, "Scientists aren't the only ones who can help bats! Everyone can! We're going to spend the day doing things that help save bats."

Plants that shouldn't be in the wild are called invasive plants. They make it hard for native plants to grow in the wild.

Native plants attract the insects that bats eat. We can pull out invasive plants and plant native species to help bats.

Bat boxes help save bats too. Many bats roost in trees. When people cut down trees, bats lose their homes. This is called habitat destruction.

To give bats a new home, we can build bat boxes! Bat boxes are sort of like birdhouses, but bats hang upside down inside.

Yaquina, 2010

Diana and Tajana were sad to leave camp, but now they had a mission. They put up bat boxes on their fences, near their school, and in their neighborhood.

OBC, 2016

At school, the two budding scientists even did a science fair project about bat conservation. Diana went to sleep every night knowing that she was doing her part to help save bats.

Action Plans

You can do things at home or in your community that can help protect bats and their environment. Here are some actions you can take.

- Build bat boxes to put on trees, barns or poles to create a home for bats.

- Leave dead trees standing in the woods. Cutting down these trees removes roosting sites for bats and other animals.

- Help out with an invasive plant removal project, and plant more native trees and shrubs. Check with local parks and land conservancy groups for locations.

Pole-mounted bat box (Haulton, 2016)

Volunteers removing invasive shrubs (McGuff, 2015)

Author's Notes

Dear Reader,

Since I was a child, I have always been interested in the "spooky" things in life. Little did I know that sometimes "spooky" things aren't scary at all. Bats fall into this category. Although bats are often portrayed in a negative light, they are actually quite cute, important, and intriguing creatures. The older I got, the more I heard about the importance of bats in keeping mosquito populations down. Unfortunately, I also heard more and more about white nose and how it is a danger to bats. This made me want to find out how I could help and now I get to do that by spreading the word about conservation and hopefully inspiring future scientists.

Alaina Page

Inquiry Activities

The following activities let you practice some of the skills used by bat researchers. To download handouts, view video clips, and more, visit the Learning Links on the Conservation Tales website: **conservationtales.com/bats**

• **Design a Bat's Ear** - design and test a bat's "ear."

• **Bat Behavior Inquiry** - Practice observation skills by taking notes about the behavior of bats.

• **Bat Box observations** - Design a bat box based on bat adaptations. Record observations about bat activity.

Bat Box Observations Data Table

Names of observers:

Observation date:

Bat box location:

Questions to investigate:

Today's weather is....
- Clear
- Cloudy
- Calm
- Partly Cloudy
- Rainy
- Windy

This bat box is located near...
- Urban (city) area
- Suburban area
- Rural area
- Park
- Farms
- Lake or pond
- River or stream
- Open fields
- Forest or woods
- Factories

Hints and Suggestions
- Note the time when you see bats leaving or entering the bat box.
- Try to count the number of bats you see.
- Look for signs of bat droppings on the bat box and on the ground under the box.
- If you can follow the bats, note where the bats appear to be feeding.

McConnell © 2017   http://www.conservationtales.com/bats.html

Conservation Tales on the Web

Find out about other books in this series, links to learning resources, and other "extras" at **conservationtales.com**

Connections to Standards

Teachers and Homeschoolers -

The table below shows the alignment of concepts and activities in this book with the Next Generation Science Standards (NGSS Lead States, 2013). Each Performance Expectation is a learning objective that reflects a Science and Engineering Practice in the context of a specific Disciplinary Core Idea that falls within a broad Crosscutting Concept. Connections to the Common Core State Standards and the Nature of Science are also listed in the yellow sections of the table.

Performance Expectations	Disciplinary Core Ideas	Science & Engineering Practices	Crosscutting Concepts
1-LS3-1: Make observation to contruct an evidence based account that young plants and animals are like, but not exacgtly like, their parents. **2-LS2-2:** Develop a simple model that mimics the function of an animal in dispersing seeds or pollinating plants. **2-LS4-1:** Make observations of plants and animals to compare the diversity of life in different habitats.	**LS2.A:** Interdependent Relationships in Ecosystems **LS3.B:** Variation of traits **LS4.D:** Biodiversity and Humans	**Asking Questions and Defining Problems** **Developing and Using Modelss** **Planning and Carrying Out Investigations** **Constructing Explanations and Designing Solutions**	**Patterns** **Cause and Effect** **System and System Models** **Structure and Function**
	Common Core State Standards Connections		**Connections to the Nature of Science**
	ELA/Literacy - 1.RI.1, W.1.7, W.1.8, W.2.7, W.2.8, SL.2.5 *Mathematics –* MP.2, MP.4, MP.5, 1.MD.A.1, 2.MD.D.10		**Science Models, Laws, Mechanisms, and Theories Explain Natural Phenomena** **Scientific Knowledge Assumes an Order and Consistency in Natural Systems** **Scientific Knowledge is Based on Empirical Evidence**

NGSS Lead States. 2013. *Next Generation Science Standards: For states, by states.* Washington, DC: National Academies Press. *www.nextgenscience.org*

Meet Our Team

Alaina Page is an Early Childhood Education student at Ball State University. She also has a minor in Natural Resources and Environmental Management and develops educational materials.

Tom J. McConnell, Ph.D., is an associate professor of Science Education in the Department of Biology, Ball State University. Dr. McConnell's teaching and research interests focus on inquiry science teaching.

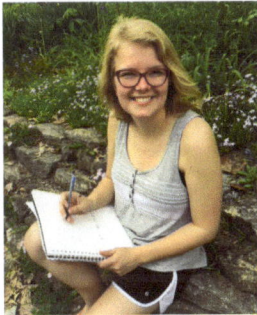

Illustrator
Sami Pfaff is a graduate from Ball State University specializing in drawing and animation. She has a special interest in drawing animals, especially birds.

Illustrator
Sierra Hensley is a graduate from Ball State University, majoring in animation. She specializes in drawing human figures.

Graphic Designer
Natalie Rokosz is a graduate from Ball State University. She loves packaging, print design, and brand design. Natalie loves animals and loves being a part of this project.

Art Director
Barbara Giorgio-Booher, MFA, is a teaching professor in the School of Art at Ball State University. She teaches drawing, figure drawing, and two-dimensional design.

Published by Airway Publishing.
Printed by Kindle Direct Publising.

Photo Credits

Photos provided by the author and content consultants except for images from Creative Commons sources. The following lists credits from the owners of the CC images.

Page	Source	License
8-9	Salmar, 2017	Pixabay
12	Organization for Bat Conservation, 2017	by permission
34	Yaquina, 2010	CC 2.0
35	Organization for Bat Conservation, 2017	by permission
37	Scott Haulton/INDR Div. of Forestry	by permission
37	Luke McGuff, 2015	CC 2.0

CC 2.0- Creative Commons license v. 2.0. See <keep same URL>.
Pixabay license. See https://pixabay.com/service/license/

For complete listing of licenses and URLs, view author contact info at **conservationtales.com**

Acknowledgments

Art Direction
Barbara Giorgio-Booher, MFA

Illustrations
Sami Pfaff
Sierra Hensley

Content Consultants
Tim Carter, Ph.D
Keifer Titus
Kristi Confortin
Aja Marcato
Amanda Bevan

Graphic Design
Natalie Rokosz

Photography
Ball State Bat Research Laboratory
Indiana DNR
Organization for Bat Research

Educational Consultant
Caitlin Zonder
   MSD of Wayne Township
   Indianapolis, IN

Special thanks to the Organization for Bat Conservation, the Hardwood Ecosystem Experiment, and Red Tail Land Conservancy for their support of bat research and conservation.

Thanks to Jameson Camp, Indianapolis, IN, for their support of Conservation Tales and inspiration for the story.

Support for the publication of this book provided by the Department of Biology, Ball State University

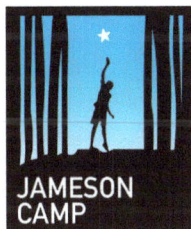

www.ingramcontent.com/pod-product-compliance
Lightning Source LLC
Chambersburg PA
CBHW060833270326
41933CB00002B/66

* 9 7 8 0 9 6 0 0 0 6 3 1 1 *